MAD MEN AND MARIGOLDS

Madeline H-Bush

For Mum.

PREFACE

Mad Men and Marigolds is my second collection of prose poetry. This collection, in my mind is an older sister to Day Drinking and Daffodils. She has experienced life and matured.

Some of these poems were born from late nights and some gut wrenching sobbing. Others are fictionalised and any resemblance to actual people living or dead, events and locales is entirely coincidental. I hope you enjoy reading them as much as I did writing them.

FBI WANNABE

I never should have looked your name up

I never should have looked at your photos.

I never should have looked through your posts.

Because if I didn't, then I wouldn't be sitting here comparing us

And questioning my entire relationship to the one you both had.

WIFI CONNECTION

With a poor connection

We talk until the early hours of the morning.

Our talks range from our day to laughing at things on the Internet

To the soft 'I love you's' as the drowsiness settles in.

I lay there,

A rare smile on my face

As I fall asleep to your voice.

BROKEN RECORD

Like a broken record,

I repeat my words.

A skip in the composition,

Playing over and over

And over and over again.

When will someone lift the needle?

A LOVER'S ANXIETY

Is this what our relationship is about? To be awake at two in the morning worrying if you made if home?

I'm angry and relieved when I finally get the text to let me know you are okay after hours of silence.

PRETTY LITTLE LIAR

Sometimes I still ask myself why you lied to me for so long when I did nothing but give you my love. Why did you string me along like a kite blowing freely in the wind? We were so close, and so happy and then you vanished on me. I'm not entirely sure why I am hurt over this years later. Maybe it is the way I reply to your messages out of the blue every so often, as if it is a life line and maybe it is also the way that captivating smile of yours tells the prettiest of lies.

IF THE WORLD
WAS ENDING

Controversial opinion; if the world was ending I know the only chance we have at redemption is women because lets face it, men would just destroy us faster with their desperation for power and control.

SNUFFED OUT

I once was a freshly dipped candle, smooth and clean. As time grew on I was lit. A burst of light on an unused wick. My flame burned bright and hot and I became everlasting, eternal and ethereal. Then you came around and grabbed the silver off of the mantle next to where I sat and snuffed out my beautiful flame, smothering it down till it could no long breathe. You close my airways and all that was left was the smoke leaving like a last breath and my wax dripping like tears. I now sit upon the mantle to gather dust and be frozen in time forever.

PRIVATE CONFESSIONS

Father, I have a confession.

Do I believe he was the definition of the right person, wrong time? Maybe I did, for a long time at least.

The breakup was never really mutual was it? Sure we had a 'mutual' breakup but I was pushed into it. I was young and stupid.

I spent years regretting it and went back and forth between old Libras and new Cancers.

When I had the opportunity to get him back I blew it by being influenced by another flame from my past. Why I listened to him? I don't know.

I guess I was disappointed in him anyway. He joined others in becoming the villain in my history, rattling my insecurity and anxiety.

I guess I can say we both never really stopped involving each other in the other's gossip though. A mutual connection always made sure to tell me that he hadn't moved on. Was I the reason? I'm not sure.

It had been three years when he reached out for the first time and what did he ask me? If there were things we could have improved in our relationship, as if I was on a free trial for a product I'd since cancelled and now had the ending questionnaire.

Now again, nearly a year on, he is being dragged back into my thoughts like a plow clearing the dirt in its path. It comes to light that he has finally found happiness. I hate to admit it but he has rocked my own.

Sometimes I lay there and I go through the long list of what ifs and wonder if I'd never listened to that girl, the one I wasn't even friends with. Would we still be together today or would things still be the same?

Father, what do I do?

POTTERY BOYS AND CLAY GIRLS

The way the Pottery Boy's hands mold the clay, running smoothly over her skin. Proud of his skills and her willingness, proof society is willing to conform women into a silent piece of art.

THE ART EXHIBITION

Pottery Boy watches from the corner as people flock around his Clay Girl, taking photos and pointing. They talk about how perfect her surface is, how smooth the curve of her side is and compare her to the goddesses in the cosmos. Pottery Boy feels nothing but pride that everyone loves his Clay Girl but now he doesn't want to share her beauty with anyone else. She's all his.

THE WHITE ROOM

The Clay Girl sits upon her pedestal, the white room is empty around her. People day in and day out come to talk about her beauty, how she's the most perfect piece of art they'd ever seen. She sees Pottery Boy talk to some of them, his smile beaming and boasting about his Clay Girl. She's silent, unable to scream out from her frozen state. Why Should Pottery boy be the voice of her existence?

CRAZY DOG LADY

I am so happy with navigating life as the Crazy Dog Lady at this point.

MAD MEN

Let me ask you the question; Why are we not burning the Mad Men at the stake for their crimes?

It's always been and will always be a witch hunt and burning for us. It makes me a Mad Woman because even though I am surrounded by the Mad Men, I am the one burning on the pyre in the town square.

FOUR O'CLOCK'S

Still trying to find someone who's willing to grow flowers in the darkest parts of me.

THE ICK

Sometimes I can't justify why I hate some of the things men do, I just hate them.

SETRALINE AMBASSADOR

Some people are destined for greatness.

I am destined for depression and daddy issues.

FBI WANNABE II

Stalking my own lovers exes.

Stalking my own exes lovers.

Either way, I am good at it.

NECESSARY SACRIFICES

Sometimes I realise I have to bleed on a stone table to give you life. It is unfortunately, a necessary sacrifice.

EMOTIONAL SUPPORT PENGUINS

Get yourself a best friend who walks around dressed like a penguin for emotional support. Those are the people you never let go of.

To my very own penguin, I love you xx

HEAVENLY DESIRE

My heart skips a beat as I watch you. Keen eyes like a snake watching her target. I trail my eyes from your sharp, jutting collar bones, to the curved plain of your shoulder down the length of your arm. I am led to veins and bones, short nails from excessive biting. I imagine those hands tracing along my skin and leaving a trail of uncontrollable fire in its wake. I imagine those hands threaded through my hair and soft lips pressing against mine. Do you know the effect you have on me? I hope not.

PRIVATE CONFESSIONS II

Father, it's me again.

Deep down I am not sure if I am cut out for relationships. I feel like I am destined to be alone.

I have never once enjoyed a relationship I have been in for long. There's always something, an excuse I conjure up that ultimately ends up hurting whoever it is I am with at the time.

Do I feel bad about it? Of course, which is why I believe I am better off alone.

Have I just not found my person yet? My soulmate?

Father, what do I do?

ON REPEAT

I cannot continue being a broken record playing to a brick wall.

WISH I HAD A DO-OVER

You weren't a waste of time but you were definitely a waste of moments.

ARE YOU STILL INTERESTED?

Not once have I been worried about a boyfriend leaving me for another woman, but today was the first time my heart stopped for a second when I saw how close you both were. Am I still good enough?

MARIGOLDS

I carry the flowers of the dead in a bouquet down the aisle to the celebration of my mistakes.

ACKNOWLEDGMENTS

Firstly, I want to thank my amazing parents, Silke and Kevin. Who need more credit sometimes for how hard they have tried to give me the best possible life. All that I am is due to the both of you.

Secondly, I'd like to thank my grandparents, Therese and Ray, and Ted and Lorraine. I feel so loved and valued by you all and can't thank you enough for all the support you have shown me in my writing.

To my Lucky, I wish you were here to celebrate this with me. Eat all the nuggets for me.

Thank you to my fur babies, Spardy, Percy, Hercules and Reuben. Percy, thank you for your little lizard tongue being there to try and clean up my tears. You made me laugh again in some of my saddest moments.

Thank you to Senura Lakmal for the beautiful cover art, you really brought it all to life.

Thank you to my beta readers, you know who you are, for this collection and suffering through

the monstrosity that was the first draft. You guys
are my ride or die and the family I chose.

A huge thank you to all my readers. Without you
all I wouldn't have the courage to do what I love.

Lastly, thank you to all the boys who have inspired
the emotions that drove these words to paper.

ABOUT THE AUTHOR

Madeline H-Bush

is an Australian writer and poet. Her entire life has been led by her love for the arts and language. Madeline is studying Literature and Creative Writing in Melbourne and lives with her parents and her three dogs Hercules, Perseus and Reuben. In her free time she loves swooning over fictional men and scrolling through social media, laughing over the whackiest of memes. Mad Men and Marigolds is second micro collection of prose poetry.